MW00533146

SPOT THE COCK

SPOT THE COCK

An Hachette UK Company
www.hachette.co.uk

Summersdale Publishers Ltd
Part of Octopus Publishing Group Limited
Carmelite House
50 Victoria Embankment
LONDON
EC4Y 0DZ
UK

www.summersdale.com

Printed and bound in China

ISBN: 978-1-78783-590-0

Substantial discounts on bulk quantities of Summersdale books are available to corporations, professional associations and other organizations. For details contact general enquiries: telephone: +44 (0) 1243 771107 or email: enquiries@summersdale.com.

SPOT
THE
COCK

A SEARCH-AND-FIND BOOK

JASON MURPHY

summersdale

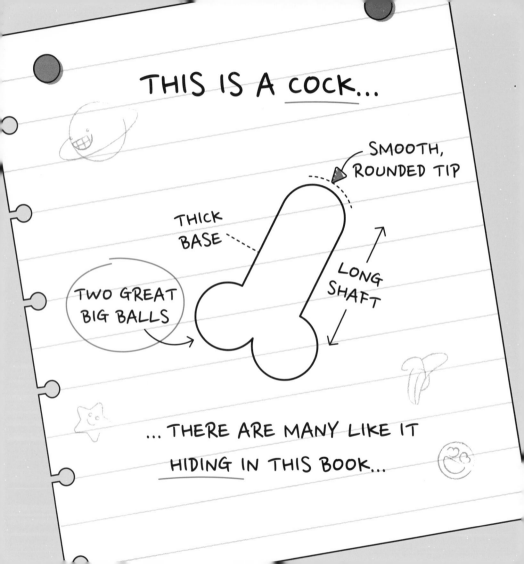

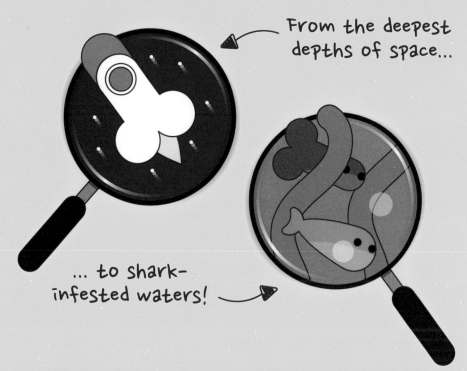

From the deepest depths of space...

... to shark-infested waters!

There's only one to find per page,
SO KEEP YOUR EYES PEELED!

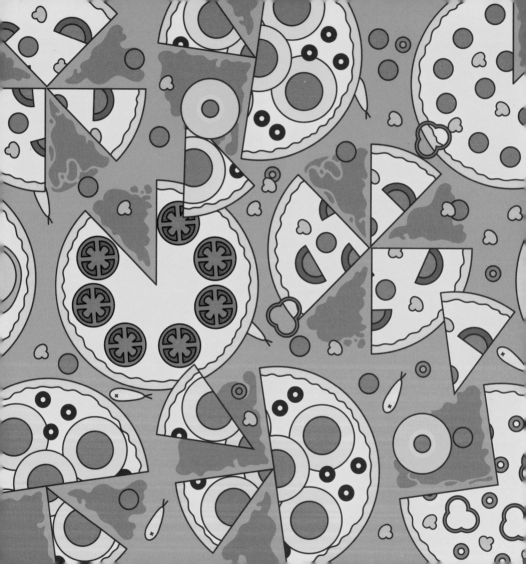

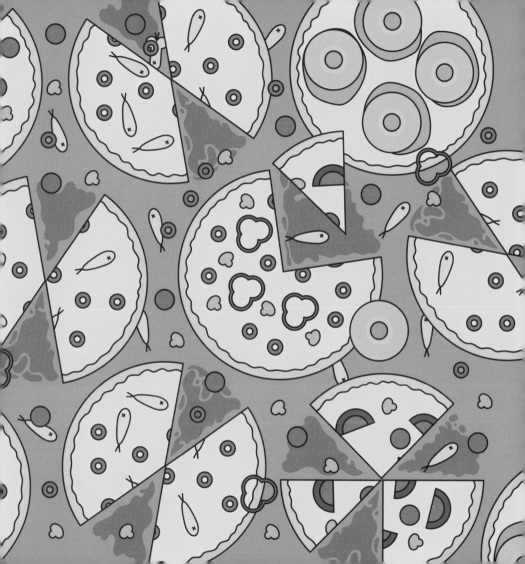

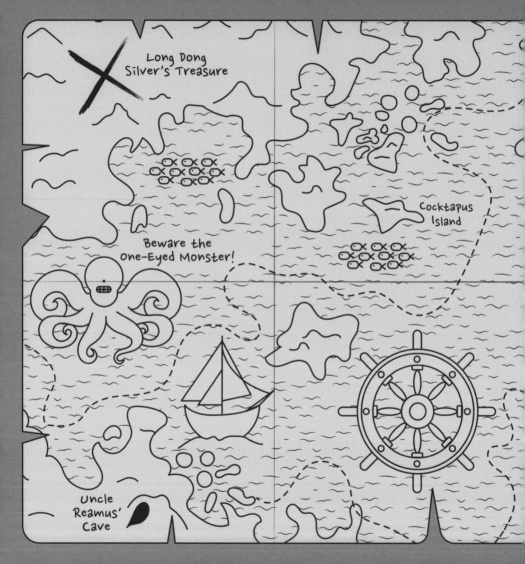

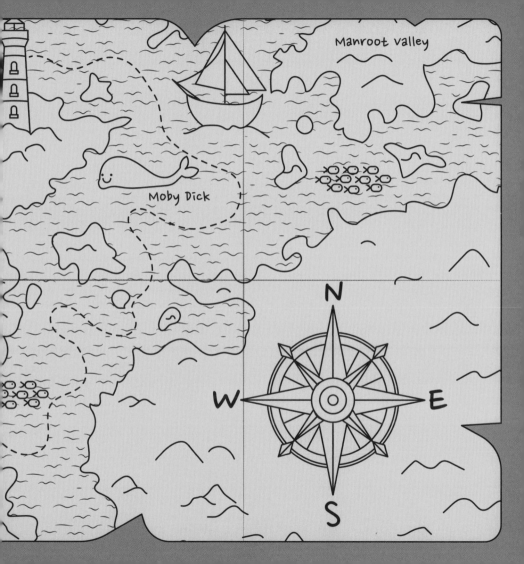

HI-SCORE 07032017

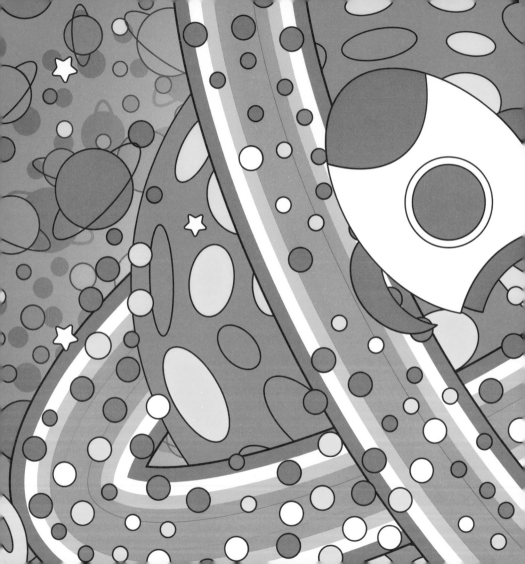

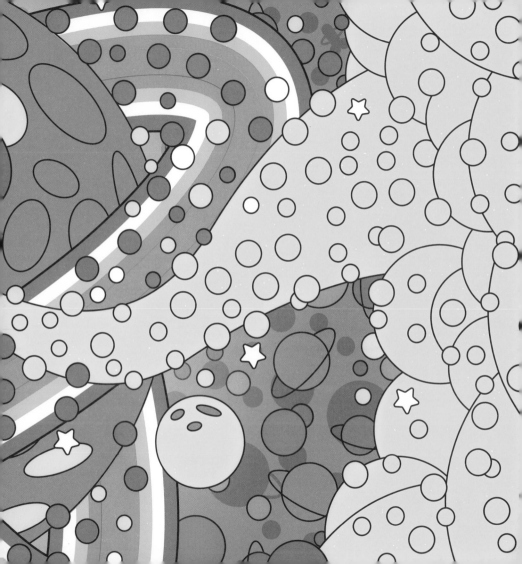

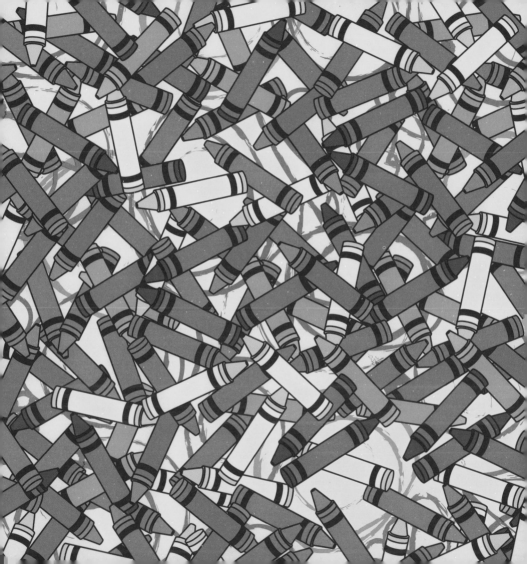

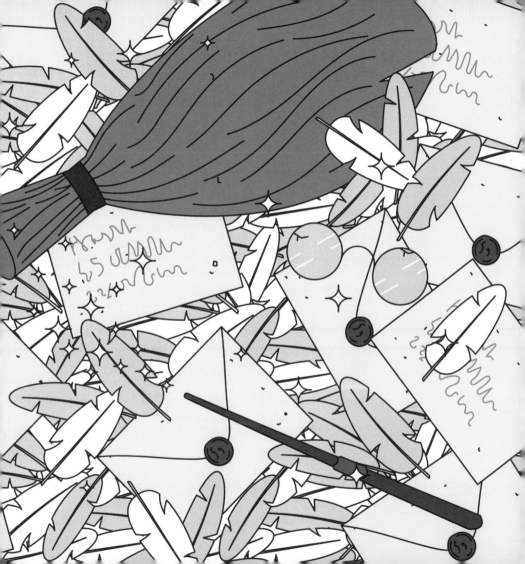

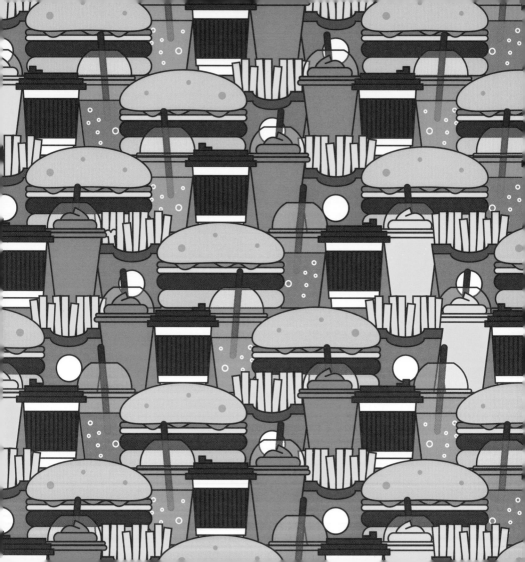

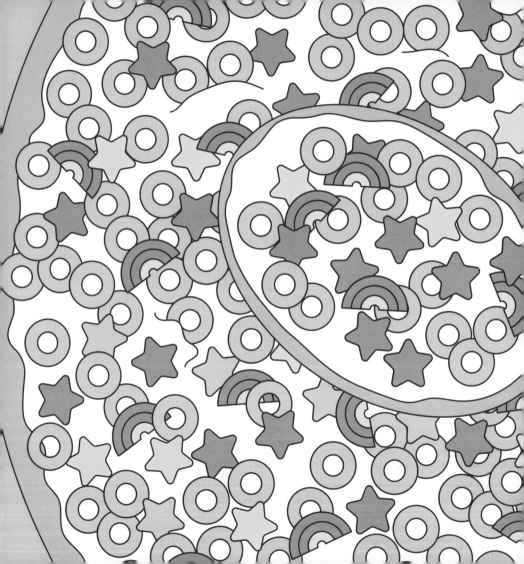

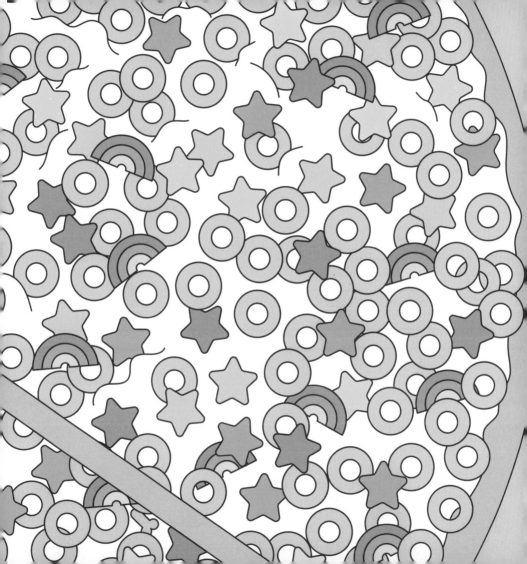

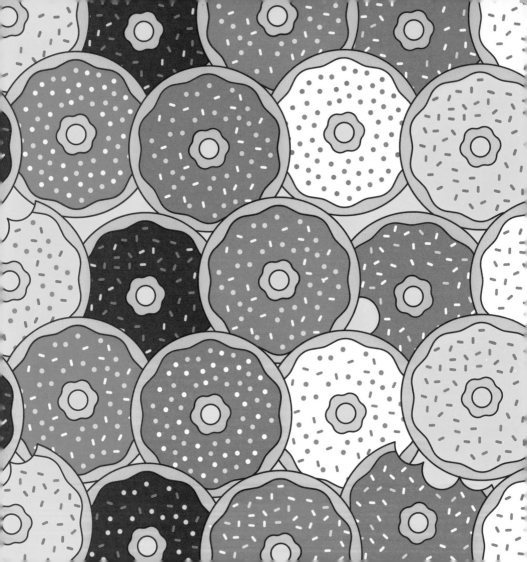

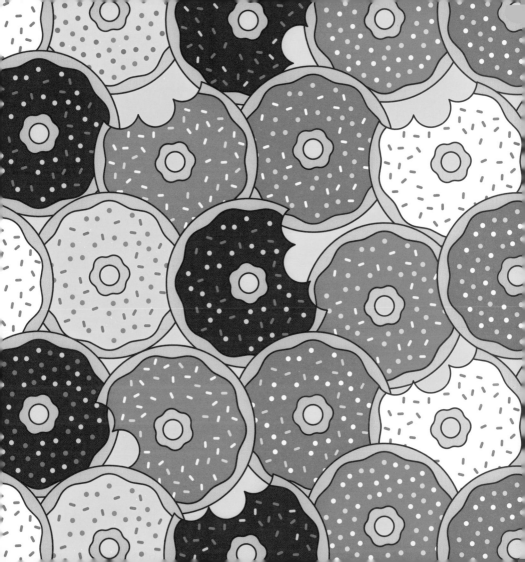

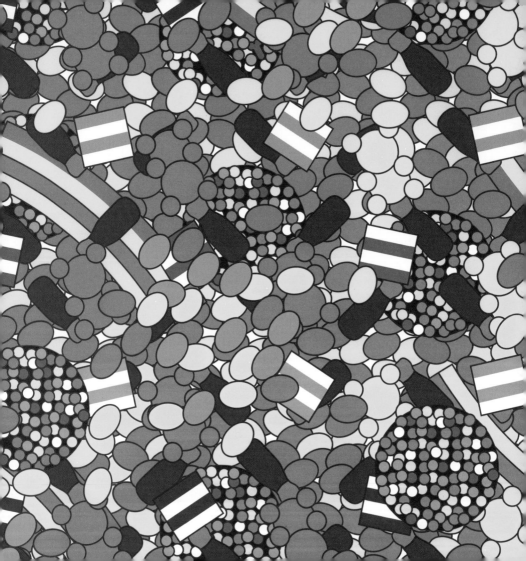

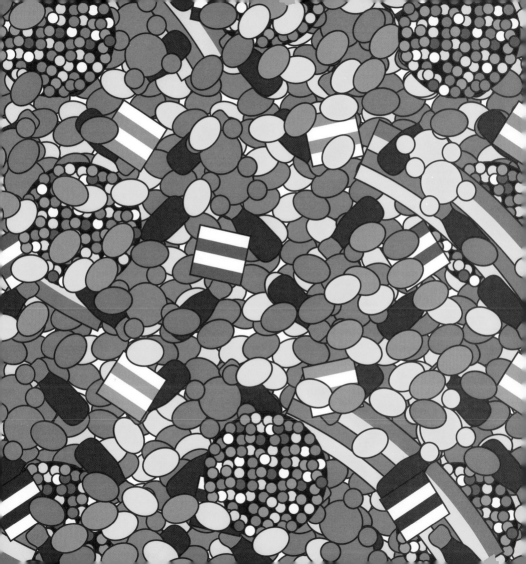

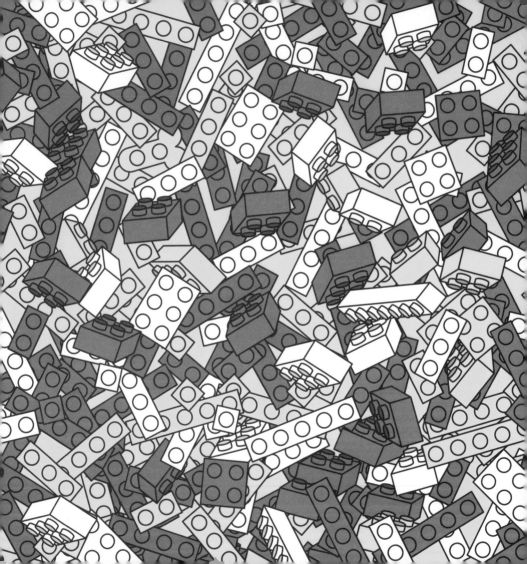

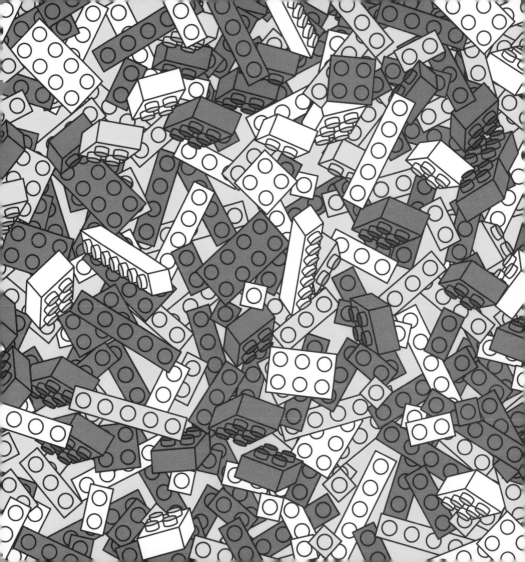

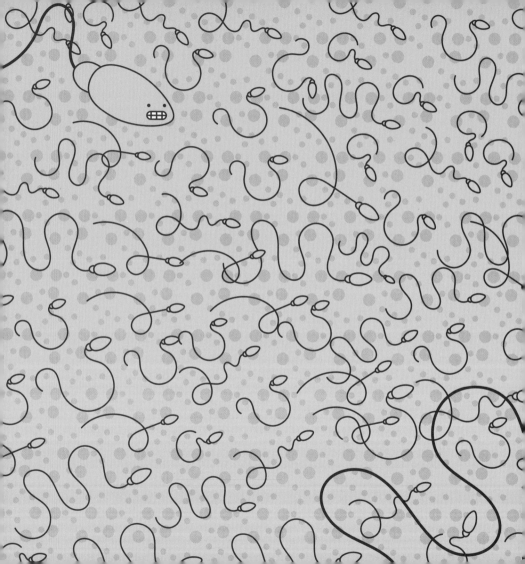

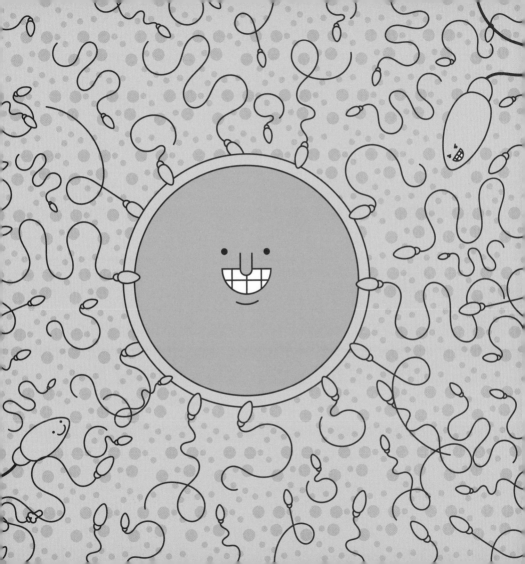

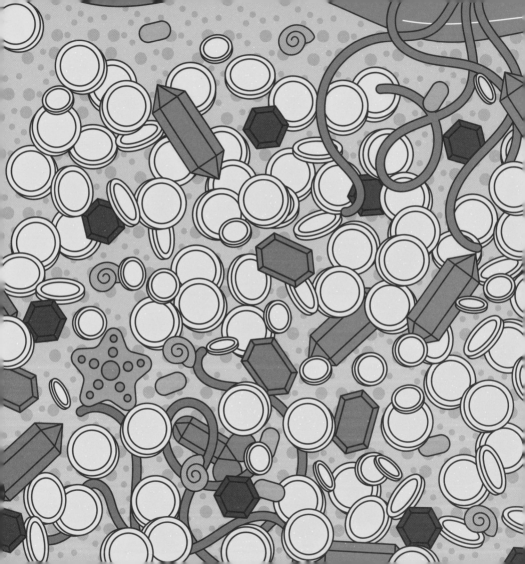

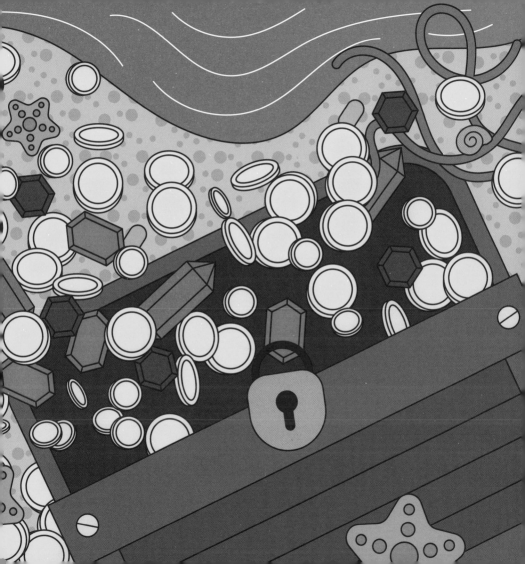

ANSWERS!

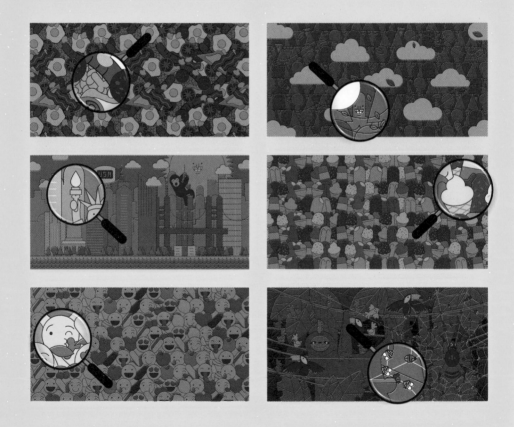

ANSWERS!

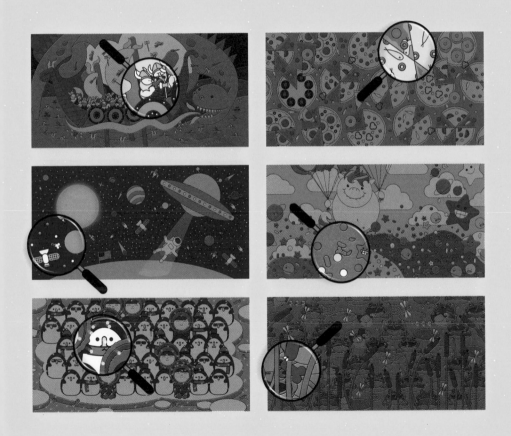

ANSWERS!

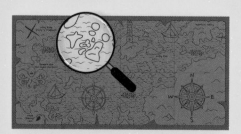

ANSWERS!

ANSWERS!

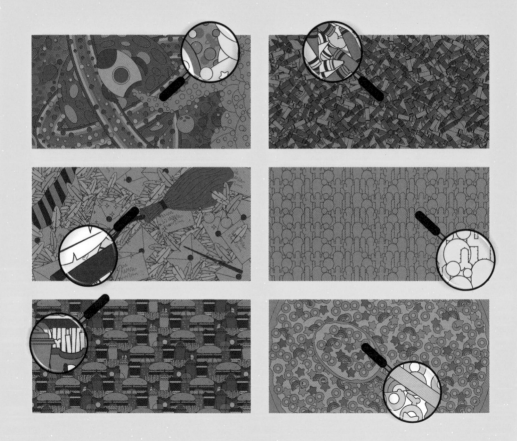

ANSWERS!

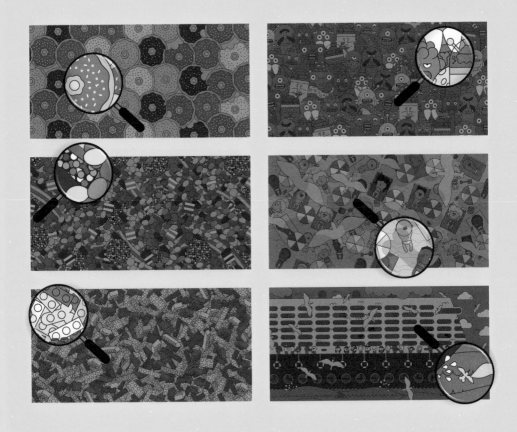

ANSWERS!

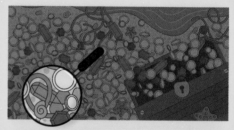

DEDICATED TO ARLO & OSCAR
(THAT'S RIGHT, I'VE DEDICATED A COCK
BOOK TO MY TWO YOUNG CHILDREN)

CHECK OUT
@JASMURPHY89
ON INSTAGRAM

If you're interested in finding out
more about our books, find us on Facebook
at Summersdale Publishers and follow
us on Twitter at @Summersdale.

www.summersdale.com